WHAT SHALL I BELIEVE?

A PRIMER OF CHRISTIAN THEOLOGY

What Shall I Believe?

A Primer of Christian Theology

By

AUGUSTUS HOPKINS STRONG
D.D., LL.D., Litt. D.

*Late President Emeritus of the Rochester
Theological Seminary*

New York   Chicago
Fleming H. Revell Company
London and Edinburgh

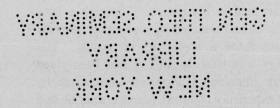
New York: 158 Fifth Avenue
Chicago: 17 North Wabash Ave.
London: 21 Paternoster Square
Edinburgh: 75 Princes Street

Introduction

JOHN the Baptist " came for witness, that he might bear witness of the light, that all might believe through him. He was not the light, but came that he might bear witness of the light." So did AUGUSTUS HOPKINS STRONG.

He was positive, for he had been convinced. He was unswerving, for he had been sent. He was persuasive, for he had been humbled and lifted up by the miraculous love of God in Christ. As a careless young student he had been arrested in his course. Through a long lifetime he had been led by a way that he knew not and made a leader of thousands. His theology was vital, because it had been given him at illuminated moments purchased by costly experience; biblical, because what he had himself felt and discovered he found again in the old-fashioned Bible, reflected, explained and foretold; unemotional, for he had followed Christ doggedly; evangelical, because having once been saved by grace he could never turn aside with would-be reformers, or lose from his

5

method the true strategy of heart-renewal as the sole cure for social ills and path to right relationships among men.

This little " *Primer* " is his valedictory. Its last words were dictated the day before the horses and chariots of fire descended. It is a charge also to all believers that remain. Two words only he wished on his tombstone : " For me to live is Christ," and " I have kept the faith." True epitaph! Many thank God upon every remembrance of him. Who follows in his train?

JOHN HENRY STRONG.

Rochester, N. Y.

Preface

MANY times of late I have been asked to put the salient points of Christian doctrine into more popular form than that of my "*Systematic Theology*." I aim in this little treatise to meet such a demand, by condensing and illustrating what I have previously written, with some additions from modern philosophy and literature.

I wish, however, to say at the very start that the truth which I present is not derived from either philosophy or literature, although I use these to throw light upon it. Before I knew much of philosophy or literature I had learned that truth, from Scripture and from my own experience. I have thought it needful, therefore, to verify my statements of Scripture by definite citations, and to help inquirers by occasional references to my own published books, in which they may find matters more fully discussed.

My allusions to personal experience run the risk of appearing too autobiographical, but I comfort myself with the example of the apostle

Paul, who found in his own heart the best con-
firmation of Scripture teaching.

Although this treatise is a Primer, in the
sense of brevity and simplicity of statement, I
cannot call it " milk for babes," for the reason
that the matters discussed are the greatest and
most profound.

I would make it a positive and constructive
statement, rather than a refutation or denunciation of false doctrine. I desire to recognize
whatever of truth there is in the theory of
evolution and in the conclusions of the higher
criticism. But I have felt bound to show that
there is a downward as well as an upward
evolution, and that the higher criticism is not
supreme arbiter in the interpretation of Scripture, but that it must be accompanied and
qualified by the insight furnished by the Spirit
of God. Modern literature furnishes us with
methods of composition which are unhistorical,
yet well fitted to convey essential truth. I have
used these to show the possibility of their use
in the composition of the Old Testament.

I hold, therefore, middle ground between the
higher critics and the so-called fundamentalists, and believe it possible for them both to
reconcile their differences by a larger view of
the deity and omnipresence of Christ. He is

" our Peace," and he holds in his girdle the key to all our problems. It is with the hope of doing something to bring about such a reconciliation, that I print this new statement of doctrine. Since my aim is above all to exalt Christ as Lord, I commend what I have done to his blessing.

AUGUSTUS H. STRONG.

Rochester, N. Y.

Contents

I

GOD IS SPIRIT

MANY years ago, when I was a pastor in Cleveland, report came to me that one of the members of my flock, superintendent of my mission-school, and professor in a medical college, was teaching his Sunday School the most arrant materialism. I invited him to a brotherly conference, and asked him what was his conception of God. He gave me an answer that would have done credit, or discredit, to a Mormon or a Swedenborgian. God, he said, was a being in human form, but of vast dimensions, spread out in space, with body like our own,—man himself, in fact, being only a miniature god.

When I reminded him that God is spirit, he replied that spirit is only a form of matter, thin and subtle, but capable of thought. I did not succeed in convincing him of his error. Dealing in his profession solely with the body, he could think only in terms of materialism: matter, space and time, were all and in all. Our conference ended in an amicable arrangement that he should resign his place as superintendent, while he still listened to my pastoral teaching as a faithful member of the church.

In all probability few of our church members have done their thinking so logically, or have carried their thinking so far. Yet I am persuaded that very many are handicapped in their Christian progress by similar misconceptions of God; and I begin my statement of doctrine by pointing out that " *God is spirit* " (John 4:24), and that this implies, not only that God has no visible form, but that he is also absolutely independent of space and time.

Spirit and Form, Space, Time

My medical friend's misconception of God was due to his wrong beginning. Dealing in his profession only with the body, he had come to believe that man is only body, and that God, in whose image man was made, must also consist only of body. He should have reflected that man is essentially spirit, and that spirit is not itself body, but that it only uses the body.

And spirit is invisible. I can never see *you,* with any outward sight: I can only see the body which you inhabit. Your inmost self, your ego, reveals itself in the play of your features and in the sound of your voice; but the cause of these changes is hidden from me;

in fact, some men put on looks so false and use words so misleading, that their real selves are quite the opposite of what they seem.

Though spirit *expresses* itself in form, it *has* no form; though it *lives* in space and time, it is not the *creature* of space and time, but is independent of them. And since knowledge of ourselves is the only clue to our knowledge of God, we conclude that spirit in God, like spirit in man, implies absence of all external form, and complete independence of space and time.

The Teaching of the Scriptures

This is the clear teaching of the Scriptures. "No man hath seen God at any time," says John's gospel (John 1:18); he is "the invisible God" (Col. 1:15); "whom no man hath seen, nor can see," says the apostle Paul (1 Tim. 6:16). Apart from his manifestations, God's being would be unknown.

Only as we penetrate into the secrets of our own being, can we understand him; and even our philosophizing goes astray, unless corrected by God's self-revelation in Jesus Christ. A part of that self-revelation is furnished us in the declaration of the book of Ecclesiastes that "God hath set eternity in our heart" (Eccl. 3:11 marg., and *Miscellanies,* 1:313-334), and in the statement of Paul that in Christ we are made "citizens of heaven" (Phil. 3:20, and *Miscellanies,* 2:159-174). As spirit in us has no form, and is invisible, so God, as pure spirit, has no body, never can be seen, yet is present everywhere and always.

There was once an atheist who tried to teach his daughter by writing on the blackboard: "GOD IS NOWHERE." But the child read it more correctly: "GOD IS NOW HERE." The doctrine of omnipresence is simply this: The whole of God is present in every place and at every time.

Modern Thought and a Spiritual God

This conception of God as spirit antedates some of the conclusions to which modern science is drifting. Einstein's "relativity" is an assertion that time and space are simply relations of material being; they have no independent existence; without matter, they cease to be. Not only Science, but also Philosophy, now sees the world to be psychic.

But a *psychic* world demands a Psyche; a universe demands a Unifier; for "psychic" means "possessed by, or manifesting, a *psyche,* or a *soul.*" The philosophy that holds to universal thought, feeling and will, while it ig-

nores or denies any soul, source or standard of truth, beauty or goodness, is like the
smile in Alice's "Wonderland," which remained, after the face to which it belonged had
disappeared.

William James well characterized such philosophy as "rotten;" by which I understand
him to mean, cut off from its source of life,
and therefore decayed, corrupt, and offensive
to God and man. If the universe is psychic,
there must be a Psyche and a Unifier. That
Psyche, that Unifier, must be a mighty *Will*,
creating, upholding, energizing all material
things; material things indeed are only the
forms of his volition, while he, as spirit, is the
invisible cause of all.

The Timeless God

This mighty Will, just yet benevolent, is
according to Scripture "King of the ages"
(1 Tim. 1:17, marg.), that is, Creator of
space and time; not subject to space and time,
but including them in his own being. With
him, not only is "one day as a thousand
years" (2 Pet. 3:8), but he lives in an
everlasting *Now*, in which all history, past,
present and future, is condensed (*Miscellanies*,
1: 313-334).

As he is essentially *Will,* we are *created*
wills, capable of a relatively independent
action, while our bodies are products of his
constant volition, and he " holdeth our soul in
life " (Ps. 66:9), even when we use these
bodies to sin against him (*" Christ in Creation,"* 30-35).

God, Personal and Triune

God is not only spirit; he is also personal.
When we apply the term personal to God,
we must not put into it any unspiritual or
materialistic meaning. God is a personal
being, because an intelligent and loving Will
is impossible without self-knowledge. The
very word " consciousness " implies duality,
a subject that knows, and an object that is
known.

But this duality of self-knowledge sometimes
becomes contrariety and insanity; a man can
hate himself and run away from himself, as
from an alien enemy. The prodigal son
" came to himself " (Lk. 15:17), and so
became normal. Duality can become fellowship, only through a third consciousness that
the two are one; and this turns the duality into
a trinity.

There are indeed instances even of a triple

consciousness within the same human personality; and the case of Dr. Jekyll and Mr. Hyde, which Robert Louis Stevenson has detailed to us, is not mere matter of a novelist's imagination. But no analogy suffices here. Three persons in one Personality constitute a union so unique that earthly analogies are only imperfect pointers toward its absolute perfection,— they simply suggest that there is nothing irrational, but rather the highest reason, in the conception that an eternal *Word* stands over against the eternal God, as his expression and counterpart; and that an eternal *Spirit* completes the self-knowledge and voluntary activity of Deity.

The personality of God, as intelligent and holy Will, implies the existence of three distinctions in his being, which are best described as three persons, and which we name Father, Son, and Holy Spirit. The Father is God unexpressed, and independent of space and time. The Son is his one and only medium of expression, his eternal object of knowledge and end in volition, his only word of communication to creatures. The Holy Spirit is the organ of fellowship; making the Trinity an infinite society of communion and love, even without the existence of creation.

Three persons are requisite, in one mighty Personality, to constitute that

> "living Will that shall endure
> When all that seems shall suffer shock;"

and a trinitarian theology is necessary, if we are to believe in a living, loving, and self-sufficient God.

Christ, the Revealer of the Father

I have already intimated that the second person of the Trinity is called not only the *Son,* but also the *Word* of God. By this last designation it is implied that he who became flesh, and who is known as Christ, is God's means of expression, not only to himself, but to creatures. In truth, we may well say that God never thinks, speaks, or acts, except through Christ.

We know the significance of *words,* in our own intercourse with others. I meet a man casually in the street. As he brushes by me, a single profane word opens to me the depths of his evil heart. A little word of kindness and compassion, from a gentle woman to a child, tells me the whole story of a mother's love. But for those words, the spirit would have been hidden. The single *word* has expressed the inmost *being*.

"In the beginning was the Word," says the prologue to John's gospel. "And the Word was with God, and the Word was God" (John 1:1, 2). In eternity past, as we may conceive it, Christ already existed as God's means of expression to himself, and as the object of his knowledge and love. It is still through his eternal Word, that God reveals himself in creation, providence, and redemption; and the whole physical universe is only the operation of Christ's will. This too is the assertion of Scripture, for John continues: "That which hath been made was life in him" (John 1:3, 4, margin).

"The Lamp Thereof is the Lamb"

Let me make this relation of Christ to the Father more plain, by citing the allusion to it in the book of Revelation. There it is said of the heavenly city, that "the glory of God doth lighten it, and the lamp thereof is the Lamb" (Rev. 21:23). God is light; but light diffused is never seen; we see *by* it, but we never see *it;* only as light is *concentrated,* is it ever *seen.* Christ, the Lamb, is the concentrated light of God; he is the Lamp, in which God's light is made visible; even in heaven, we shall never see the Father, except as he is expressed in Jesus Christ.

And so our Lord himself says to Philip: " He that hath seen *me*, hath seen the Father; how sayest thou: Show us the Father? " (John 14: 9). And Paul sees "the light of the knowledge of the glory of God " only " in the face of Jesus Christ " (2 Cor. 4: 6); while the author of the Epistle to the Hebrews speaks of Christ as " the effulgence of God's glory and the very image of his substance " (Heb. 1: 3).

All the light of God is concentrated in Jesus Christ, so that he is the only God with whom we have to do; he is God manifest in the flesh (1 Tim. 3: 16); in him is all the fullness of the Godhead bodily (Col. 2: 9) ; in him are hid all the treasures of wisdom and knowledge (Col. 2: 3).

Andrew Fuller once said that the doctrines of theology were " united together like chain-shot, so that, whichever one enters the heart, the others must certainly follow." This is peculiarly true with regard to our view of Christ; and what I have said of him will determine and dominate my whole subsequent treatment of theology (Matt. 22: 42).

II

CHRIST IN CREATION

AS the Father expresses himself in the Son, so the Son expresses himself in creation; first, in the creation of what we call matter; and secondly, in the creation of intelligent beings.

This is not a creation out of nothing, as some have imagined; for out of nothing, nothing can come. It is rather the differentiation of his one infinite Will into myriads of finite wills. We speak of Shakespeare as "myriad-minded;" but Christ's resources are infinitely greater than those of Shakespeare, for Christ is "made priest . . . after the power of an endless life" (Heb. 7: 16).

The simile of light may help us here also. Every ray of light may be divided into all the colors of the solar spectrum. So Christ, the Light of the world, may be said to express himself in all the works of his hands. His mighty Will may show its power in myriads of finite wills, some intelligent, some unintelligent, some spiritual, some material.

Modern science is coming to the conclusion

that what we call matter is only centres of
force; and that force is simply *will* in action.
How else explain the fact of gravitation, the
action of each particle of matter upon every
other, so that my throwing of a ball into the
air attracts the whole earth and, if not counteracted by other forces, causes the whole universe to move?

" A distinguished philosopher has said that
every body in the solar system is behaving as
if it knew precisely how it ought to behave in
consistency with its own nature, and with the
behavior of every other body in the same
system. . . . Each atom has danced countless
millions of times, with countless millions of
different partners, many of which required an
important modification of its mode of motion,
without ever departing from the correct step or
the right time." The whole universe, from
centre to circumference, is alive, and its life is
Christ (John 1: 3, 4, margin; *Miscellanies,*
1: 220-238).

The Universe and Christ

So we claim that something more than atoms
is needed to explain the universe. A correlat-
ing Intelligence and Will must be assumed.
Atoms by themselves would be like a heap of

loose nails, which need to be magnetised, if they are to hold together. All structures would be dissolved, and all forms of matter would disappear, if the Presence that sustains them were withdrawn. The atom, like the monad of Leibnitz, is *parvus in suo genere deus*—" a little god in its nature "—only because it is the expression of the mind and will of an *immanent* God.

And that immanent God is Christ. The creation of matter is only the beginning of his volitions in space and time, under the law of cause and effect. Matter is Christ's self-limitation under the law of necessity. Humanity is Christ's self-limitation under the law of freedom. Incarnation and Atonement are Christ's self-limitations under the law of grace.

In Christ " all things consist," or hold together (Col. 1 : 17) : in short, his living will is the glue which keeps the universe, and all that it contains, from disintegration and annihilation.

The creation of *mind* is only his adding to the bodies of his creatures a freedom of intelligent control which makes them relatively independent, capable of virtue, and therefore responsible.

While the eternal Word is unlimited before

creation, and, after creation, is limited only by
his own volition, man's self-knowledge and
self-control are subject to such change and
growth as are required by the conditions of
space and time.

Trinity and Humanity

I cannot leave this part of my subject without pointing out that there is a relation,
hitherto seldom suspected, between the trinitarian element in man and the trinitarian
element in God.

As man lives, moves, and has his being only
in God (Acts 17:28), created spirits can
know themselves and have fellowship with one
another only by participating in what we may
call the natural life of the Godhead.

For as there is a natural activity of the
Word, in all human consciousness and moral-
ity; and as Christ before his incarnation was
in all men the principle of science, law, benevo-
lence, progress; so the Holy Spirit was the
principle of unity and fellowship, revealing to
man the depths of his own being, and the sub-
lime nature of his relations to God.   Even
before his incarnation, Christ was the Light
that lighteth every man (John 1:9); and the
Holy Spirit, even before he could reveal the

crucified and risen Christ (John 7:39), was the persuader of social, national, and universal peace, the real author of all unity, organization and law (Gen. 1:2).

Creatorship and Lordship

Let us pause to consider how completely this view of Christ's creatorship makes him Lord of all. Nature is not only "the living garment of the Deity," as Gœthe declares, but it is the living garment of Christ. It is the same hand that was stretched out on the cross for our redemption that paints the sunset clouds with beauty, and directs the tides of life on the far shores of the universe. It is Christ who by his indwelling in humanity gives solidarity to the race, and in spite of its sin ensures its civilization and progress.

Separate races and separate men may seem at first sight to have no connection with one another; but they are like islands of the sea which the waters hold apart, but which are bound to one another by a rocky foundation under all the currents of the ocean. Because we are "God's offspring" (Acts 17:28, 29), we have a natural oneness with all men in Christ, which antedates and prepares the way for Christian unity and fellowship.

All the appearances of God in the Old Testament from Abraham to Isaiah were appearances of Christ (John 8:56; 12:41). He thundered from Sinai when he gave the law, long before he preached the sermon on the Mount of Galilee. The Rock that followed Israel through the desert and gave the people drink was really Christ (1 Cor. 10:4).

Every voice of conscience that has ever spoken to us was his voice. Every breath we draw is by use of powers with which he has endowed us, and which he sustains. Every heart-beat is a testimony to his personal presence and activity within our physical frame.

" Whither shall I go from thy Spirit, or whither shall I flee from thy presence? If I ascend into heaven, thou art there; if I make my bed in Sheol, behold, thou art there " (Ps. 139:7, 8). And this ever-present God of whom the Psalmist speaks is none other than the Redeemer against whom we have sinned, and who seeks to reveal himself within us for our salvation. How plain it is that there is " none other name under heaven that is given among men whereby we may be saved " (Acts 4:12)!

Christ and the Individual

Christ is the ground of all individual existence. This I have illustrated by the underlying foundation for all the seemingly separate islands of the sea. We live, move and have our being in Christ, because he is the only expression of God. All our natural life is derived from him, and is shared by him, and the only exception is our will to do evil.

Modern psychology makes much of subliminal consciousness. This we may believe to be the peculiar element of Christ's activity and control. A thousand impulses to good come to us unsought. Dreams encourage us. Childhood and youth are blest with aspirations and ideals beyond the parent's power to explain. Wordsworth has well said that "Heaven lies about us in our infancy." But ordinary men are like islands in which a single slumbering volcano rears its head. Consciousness in them registers only occasional impulses of their better nature.

Jesus was the *only-begotten* Son of God, so that in him the subliminal and the conscious activity become practically one. Limited as his earthly knowledge was, of the day and the hour of the end (Matt. 24: 38), he knew what was of far greater importance, namely, all things that the Father was doing (John 5:20), and the fact that he and the Father were one (John 10:30). It was by the disclosure, to himself and to the world, of the infinite resources of his own being, that he was able to teach the truth, to work miracles, to retake his life after he had laid it down (John 10:17).

The difference between Christ and common men is two-fold: first, that his life is the *source* of all other lives, while our life is only *derived* from him; and secondly, that in him was " all the *fulness* of the Godhead bodily " (Col. 2:9) while common men are only *sparks* from the divine flame.

Sanday of Oxford has made this possession of the divine fulness, in the subliminal consciousness of Christ, to be the explanation both of his absolute authority and of his earthly. limitations (*Systematic Theology,* 2:699, 700; *Miscellanies,* 1:478-493). We can accept this suggestion of Sanday, if we clear it from all implication of pantheism by saying that in nature Christ is not only immanent, but also *transcendent* (Job. 26:14); that the human soul, in spite of Christ's furnishing its powers, can use those powers to thwart the purpose of the Creator; and that humanity has actually, by its sin, so infected this subliminal source of good that it has become instead a constant source of evil, to be counteracted by providence and to be overcome by regeneration. This is the doctrine of original sin, in which we go further than Sanday.

We also maintain that, since Christ is the manifested God (1 Tim. 3: 16), he is so identified with our humanity that he can suffer *for,* and *in,* each one of us, as fully as if the whole Godhead were engaged in the work of our salvation. God is free from all limitations of space and time. His omnipresence is the presence of the whole of God in every place. In Christ he is the inmost life of every human soul. In Christ he can therefore be the suffering, yet the blessed God; and our atoning Savior can also be our final Judge. In short, we have, in Christ, God's complete and final self-revelation (Is. 63: 9; 1 Tim. 1: 11; *Miscellanies,* 2:310-328).

All Things Summed up in Christ

Christ is the God of nature, the God of history, the God of Scripture, the God of the church, the God of the individual soul. Robert

Browning saw God's face in the whole universe when he wrote:

> "That one Face, far from vanish, rather grows,
>   Or decomposes but to recompose,
>   Become my universe that feels and knows,"

and he explains his meaning when he says: "That Face is the face of Christ." This explanation clears his poem from all charge of pantheism, and sets the poet side by side with Jonathan Edwards, as teaching the deity and omnipresence of Christ.

Pantheism has no real Christ, and no personal God. The God of pantheism is a God conterminous with the universe and imprisoned within it; while the real Christ is transcendent as well as immanent, not only "in all" and "through all", but also "above all" (Eph. 4:6).

Pantheism knows no more personality in man than in God; while the creatures of the personal Christ are personal beings made in God's image, free and responsible. Pantheism makes men automata, subjects only of the law of cause and effect; while Christ's human creatures are free to serve or to rebel, to choose heaven, or to choose hell.

So our Christ, the Christ of Scripture, as

our manifested God, gives us the only clue to the mysteries of the universe, and to the problems of theology. "Oh the depth of the riches both of the wisdom and the knowledge of God! . . . For of him, and through him, and unto him, are all things" (Rom. 11:33, 36; "*Christ in Creation,*" 1-14).

III

HOLINESS AND SIN

THE fundamental attribute of God is holiness. Holiness is self-affirming purity. In virtue of this attribute God eternally wills and maintains his own moral excellence. Justice and righteousness are only forms in which holiness manifests itself.

Holiness is not self-communicating love, but rather self-affirming righteousness. Holiness limits and conditions love; for love can will happiness, only as happiness results from, or consists with righteousness, that is, with conformity to God.

All non-conformity to God in moral relations is sin; and sin is hateful in God's sight, for it is not only the enemy and destroyer of all purity and peace, but it is in itself the opposite of the right, the true and the good. God therefore attaches suffering to sin, as its proper penalty, even though he himself shares in that suffering, as the Creator and Life of the sinner.

Holiness Absolute in its Requirement

To prefer any subordinate good to God, the

source and standard of all good, is sin.   It is
sin because it worships the creature rather than
the Creator.

Even truth, beauty and goodness are not to
be sought apart from him who is himself truth,
beauty and goodness.   The real aim of one
who prides himself upon making Truth his
supreme object is such a rearrangement of the
universe as will enable him to escape the restraints of God's holiness and to fancy himself
a thinker greater than God.   This is once more
the rotten philosophy of self-interest, which
explains Christianity by its own principle of
supreme regard for happiness.

To this philosophy Christianity is a protest.
The book of Job is a demonstration that man
may serve God without regard to his own interest ("Though he slay me, yet will I trust in
him," Job 13 : 15).   Jesus is our highest example of right doing, when right doing leads
to death ("Not my will, but thine, be done,"
Luke 22 : 42).

And I, myself, at my conversion, found no
peace until I had given up all desire for peace.
I had sought the Lord apparently in vain.   I
was going back to College unconverted.   My
father came to the train, disconsolate because
I was going back to my ungodly companions

with no evidence that I was a Christian. I clambered into the car with the words ringing in my ears, " The harvest is past, the summer is ended and my soul is not saved." The conductor said, " All aboard," and the train left the station. I said to myself, " This train is taking me to hell! " I leaned my head on top of the seat in front of me and began to think: " Why have I failed? It must be because I have been making an experiment of this thing. God wants a finality. I have been thinking that if I did not succeed, I could go back. God wants my service, not because it will bring me peace or happiness, but because that service is my bounden duty, and because he is my rightful Lord." Then I resolved to serve God only, whether I lived or died, even if I never heard a word from his lips of pardon or comfort.

And that is my protest against the Epicurean doctrine that Christianity is simply a choice of God for the sake of happiness. There is no virtue in seeking truth apart from God: it is idolatry rather, like the sin that esteems the works of God's hands as objects of greater devotion than is God himself; nor can such seekers of truth claim any merit in their so-called independence. However noble may be

the stoical character, and however prolonged
the quest, it is like the electric lamp held
against the sun,—through the smoked glass
of the astronomer it becomes a black spot
upon that blazing disk. The law of God
makes all our self-righteousness to be sin, and
puts the whole world under condemnation,
" for through the law cometh the knowledge
of sin " (Rom. 3 : 20).

Sin's Nature Seen in its Consequences

Years ago I stood on the deck of an ocean
steamer, listening to the talk of the captain. A
steward came suddenly forward and told the
captain that a hostler, in charge of horses in
the hold, had thrown a lighted match into the
straw, and that the men near found difficulty
in putting out the blaze. The captain turned
pale, rushed to the gangway, seized the of-
fender by the collar, dragged him from the
stall, and put him in irons for the rest of the
voyage. And all for throwing away a lighted
match? Yes, because that lighted match might
have meant the loss of the ship a thousand
miles from land, and the drowning of all her
passengers and crew. The captain hated fire.

The fire that God hates is sin. The least
sin is self-multiplying. Left to itself, it will

set on fire the whole course of nature, and it
is itself set on fire by hell (James 3:6).

God has permitted sin to begin in so small a
way, in order that its evil may be the more
manifest. How small a thing seemed the first
transgression—the eating of the fruit of the
forbidden tree!

> "'Twas but a little drop of sin
> We saw this morning enter in;
> And lo, at eventide, the world is drowned!"

A single flesh-fly, with its progeny in the
tropics, will devour a sheep's carcass as quickly
as will a lion. Sin is a principle in course of
development. Do not judge it by what it is
now, but by what it may become. Its small
beginnings hide an infinity of evil.

We can stamp out tuberculosis only at the
start; when it is developed, there is no cure,
and no staying of its ravages. And sin is
plausible and deceitful at the beginning; it even
comes to us as an angel of light (2 Cor.
11:14); but, " when it is full-grown, it bring-
eth forth death" (James 1:15). Therefore,
God, who sees the future in the present, cries
to us, with most pathetic voice: " O, do not
this abominable thing, that I hate!" (Jer.
44:4).

Sin's Consequences to Christ

And Christ was "the Lamb slain from the foundation of the world" (Rev. 13:8), because even from the beginning he suffered for human sin.

Can a father see his daughter the victim of a betrayer, lost to purity, and going down to death, without shame and agony that blanch the hair and paralyze the heart? Christ saw ten thousand cases like that; aye, the whole mass and weight of the world's sin and sorrow fell on him, till not only beads of sweat stood upon his brow, but the very blood was forced through the pores and fell in great drops upon the ground. All this, with the darkened heavens and the broken heart of the cross—these were not simply Christ's sufferings,—they were *God's* also; and the apostle does not hesitate to speak of the church of God which he purchased with his own blood" (Acts 20:28), for Christ's blood was the blood of God (*Miscellanies,* 2:340-359).

Sin the Negation of God

And yet the dreadful consequences of sin are not the main reason why God hates it. He hates it because it is the *opposite of his nature.*

In itself, and apart from its consequences, it is condemnable.

As you abhor dirt, filth, lust, cruelty, hypocrisy, so God abhors sin. It is rebellion over against his sovereignty; darkness, over against his light; impurity, over against his purity; selfishness, over against his love.

Sin is his antagonist and would-be destroyer. Sin would dethrone God, and set up its own rule upon the ruins of God's empire. Sin is the effort of the creature to take the place of the Creator; of the planet to make itself the centre of the solar system; of finite man to "oppose and exalt himself against all that is called God or that is worshipped; so that he sits in the temple of God, setting himself forth as God" (2 Thess. 2:4). All sin is the attempt, consciously or unconsciously, to secure what Satan promised in his first temptation, namely, "Ye shall be as God" (Gen. 3:5).

Sin the Background of Grace

But God aims to show, not only the greatness of sin, but the *greatness of Christ*. If sin abounds, grace abounds much more (Rom. 5:20). As the ship captain starts to extinguish the blaze, so Christ leaves his throne, and endures the cross, that he may put down sin in this revolted province of his empire. It is a revelation to principalities and powers in heavenly places, as well as to mortal man. So he may preserve other worlds from falling, and the sad experience of our planet may work out the lasting good of the entire universe. This little sphere, though it is not the material centre, may yet be the spiritual centre, of God's whole system of worlds. Here is enacted the greatest drama of the ages. And the most important thing in history is the Cross,

> "Where Christ, the mighty Maker, died
> For man, the creature's, sin."

Let us estimate our own sins by *God's standard*. Let us see in the least of them the beginnings of infinite evil. Let us fly to Christ as our refuge from their guilt and power.

Sin and God's Plan of Recovery

The one object of God's self-revelation in creation is to restore in man the image and likeness of God by making him a son, in union with Christ's sonship, and by giving him experience of his own greatness, in the reception of Christ's Spirit.

For man, as we have seen, is essentially, not

matter, but spirit. Like God himself, he can exist without body, and freed from the limitations of space and time. But being a finite, and not an infinite spirit, he can enter into this rest and dominion, only through growth and education.

He must learn the alphabet before he can read, and must master the multiplication-table before he can use the calculus. Space and time, with the limitations of a material body, are the necessary conditions of this education.

And especially, the possession and exercise of free-will are necessary for moral development and progress. Without freedom man's obedience to law would be merely automatic and mechanical. Power to do evil must exist, if there is to be any virtue in doing good. And God submits to the sorrow and suffering, which are the penalty of disobedience in his creatures, only because he can share that sorrow and suffering with them, and can make these evils the means of their restoration. The holiness of God, which punishes sin by its consequences of misery, has for its first effect his own suffering, so that God himself is the greatest sufferer of the universe (Gen. 6:6; Jer. 44:4; Is. 63:9).

The End Foreseen from the Beginning

God's plan, from the very beginning and before the beginning, included the permission of man's fall, together with the provision for his recovery.

The first man was a child, but he was not a savage. He was undeveloped, but he had right intuitions and inclinations, and he was free to choose between good and evil.

In the exercise of freedom, he might have chosen the path of upward progress; but he chose to take the downward road; and evolution may be downward toward hell, instead of upward toward heaven.

We have numberless instances of animal species which have deteriorated and have finally gone out of existence; indeed, those which have perished outnumber the survivors a hundred to one. Herbert Spencer tells us that " retrogression has been as frequent as progression." And Tennyson contrasts the two tendencies in his couplet :

" Evolution, ever climbing after some ideal good,
  And Reversion, ever dragging Evolution in the mud."

Is the world growing better? Yes, but it is also growing worse. Every increase of goodness makes evil more intense in its opposition.

The free-will of man counteracts his upward growth in the arts, in science, and even in civilization, though these are proofs that the Spirit of Christ is still working in him.

A very high artistic and poetic development may coexist with great moral degradation; as in the days of Raphael and the Borgias, when a pope could have his paramour painted for an altar-piece representing the Virgin.

In my essay on "Degeneration" (*Miscellanies,* 2: 110-128), I have quoted the conclusions to which men of broad understanding have come with regard to the beginnings of the human race. "Cannibalism and infanticide," says Gulick, "are unknown among the anthropoid apes. These must be the results of degradation. Pirates and slaveholders are not men of low and abortive intelligence, but men of education, who deliberately throw off all restraint, and who use their powers for the destruction of society." "There is no cruel treatment of females among animals," says Mark Hopkins. "If man came from the lower animals, then he cannot have been originally savage, for you find the most of this cruel treatment among savages," and not among the lower animals.

The apostle Paul, in the first chapter of his

Epistle to the Romans, has given us the key to history, when he declares that primitive man knew God, but glorified him not as God; that he exchanged the truth of God for a lie, and in consequence was given up to a reprobate mind (Rom. 1:18-32); and John declares that this degeneration can be counteracted only by regeneration from above (John 3:3).

Holiness Vanquishing Sin

If what I have said thus far is true, we should regard human history as God's evolution of his plan for man's redemption through the work of Christ and of the Holy Spirit, which culminated in the suffering of the cross and the founding of the church. Little by little God has revealed himself, as the world has been able to bear it. Only in the fullness of time could the incarnation take place (Gal. 4:4); for, until man knew himself to be a lost sinner, there was no propriety in proclaiming to him salvation.

Only to a chosen nation and to a prepared people could the clear prophecy of a Redeemer be given, while other peoples had only scattered rays of the true light (Rom. 3:1). Yet God did not leave himself without a witness in any land (Acts 14:17). Confucius and Buddha and Zoroaster were his partial agents, doing a little to reform evil systems and to improve moral conditions. Mixed with error as their teachings were, the coin they furnished had more of lead in it than silver; and the washing of silver that gave it currency did not prevent it from being a counterfeit of the true, nor from making its authors "thieves and robbers," when their doctrine stole the hearts of men away from Christ (John 10:8).

When Christ himself comes in human form, he sums up all the truth of these partial revelations, and adds his personal testimony and example, to show that in him man may come to union and fellowship with the infinite God.

The Holy Spirit who has put eternity into our heart (Eccl. 3:11; *Miscellanies,* 1:313-331), lifts us up at times to see things from God's point of view, *sub specie aeternitatis.* Inspiration, indeed, may be only the reinforcement of a faculty normal to sinless man, but which he has lost by transgression; and the prophets were men who "searched what time or what manner of time the *Spirit of Christ* which was in them did signify, when it testified beforehand the sufferings of Christ, and the glories that should follow them" (1 Pet. 1:11).

So we have in human history a downward evolution caused by man's sin, side by side with an upward evolution due to the presence in humanity of the life-giving Christ. The tares and the wheat grow together till the time of the harvest (Matt. 13 : 30). Then the tares shall be cast into the furnace of fire, but the wheat shall be gathered into God's storehouses. The holiness of God shall at last be vindicated. The Cross of Christ on the one hand, and on the other hand the heaven or hell which follow its acceptance or rejection, show God's estimate of sin.

IV

CHRIST AND SCRIPTURE

WE come now to the consideration of Christ's relation to Holy Scripture. The whole matter is summed up in the statement that *the written word is the expression of the eternal Word.*

But as the eternal Word was made flesh and appeared in human form, so the written word comes to us through the weak and halting methods of human composition. As the Father expressed himself in Christ under the limitations of space and time, beginning as a mere speck in the womb of the Virgin, coming to the full consciousness of his dignity and mission as he grew in stature and wisdom, and learning obedience by the things which he suffered, so Christ expressed himself gradually in the Scriptures, beginning with the prophecy that the seed of the woman should bruise the serpent's head (Gen. 3 : 15), enlarging the revelation by occasional theophanies and by the types of the Mosaic service, by the rough denunciations of the herdsman Amos and the surpassing eloquence of the courtier Isaiah, until at last, in his personal manifestation in human form, he furnished the key to all the past and made God understood to all the future (John 1: 17, 18).

Scripture a Superintended Evolution

After what I have said of Christ, as the life and light of men, I can speak without hesitation of the evolution of Scripture. Evolution is simply the *ordinary* method of Christ's working. He uses the past in his building of the future, as he uses the seed in his bringing forth of fruit (Gen. 1: 12).

But this method is not exclusive. It leaves room for absolute creation, for incarnation, miracle, resurrection; indeed, these are required either to precede, explain, or supplement the evolutionary process. Christ can work from within, as easily as from without (Gal. 1: 16). There need be no denunciation of an evolutionary element in the composition of Scripture, so long as we recognize to the full that holy men of old wrote as they were moved by the Spirit of Christ (1 Pet. 1: 11; 2 Pet. 1: 21).

In this evolution of Scripture, Christ may use all the methods of literary composition

which are consistent with truth—poetry as
well as prose, proverb as well as history, parable as well as dogmatic teaching, apologue
and drama as well as legislative enactment.
Even hyperbole and fable are found in the
Old Testament (Deut. 1:28; Judg. 9:14).
This variety of method has given such interest and popularity to the Bible that it has
become the most widely circulated book of the
world.

Christ's revelation may be a progressive one,
requiring a final and personal appearance of
the Lawgiver, to show the connection of its
parts and to disclose the meaning of the whole.
But because one mighty Spirit of Christ has
breathed through the whole process of Scripture growth from the beginning to the end,
Christian experience recognizes the written
word as the expression of the eternal Word,
and, when taken as a whole and rightly interpreted, the supreme rule of our faith and
practice.

The Function and Limits of Criticism

The higher criticism has its rights, and we
must concede that it has thrown valuable light
upon the methods employed in the composition
of Scripture. But the higher criticism is not

master, but servant, of our spiritual sense; and its surmises must bow to the total testimony of the word of God.

The Bible is given for the use and comprehension of ordinary Christians; the same Spirit that inspired the Bible is given to Christ's followers to interpret what he has permitted to be written; and each Christian is to be judged at the last day by his obedience or disobedience to the plain teaching of the Bible.

The confessions of faith which have marked the history of the church show clearly that the great majority of believers have found Scripture to teach the deity and pre-existence of Christ, his incarnation, virgin birth, miracles, vicarious atonement, physical resurrection, his omnipresence in the hearts of his people, and his final coming to be Judge of the living and of the dead.

The Bible a Divinely Edited Literature

The Bible is, therefore, not simply *revelation;* it is also *literature.* Not all of it is divine dictation; most of it is human utterance. The relation of Scripture to Christ, as its principal author, enables us to interpret many problems which would otherwise be insoluble.

For Christ was the Word of God made flesh.

The written word which expresses him is
therefore the word of God made human;
adapted to ordinary human comprehension;
limited by many shortcomings and imperfec-
tions. It is a record of man's downward
progress, in spite of Christ's restraints and in-
centives to obedience. " By diverse portions
and in diverse manners " (Heb. 1:1), and
usually through man's own reports, though
selected and supervised by Christ, it tells the
story of the downward progress of the human
race until man's sin culminated in the effort to
murder man's Creator, and to quench in darkness man's only Light.

That record of sin must be taken as a whole,
gathered as it was from human life and from
conflicting sources. No single utterance can
be taken as complete truth; it must be taken in
connection with its context; like the railway
coupon, it is " not good if detached." The
sentence, " There is no God " must have its
explanation from the words that precede it—
" The fool hath said in his heart " (Ps. 14:1).
The Old Testament must be taken in connection with the New, and the words of Jesus in
connection with the later words of his apostles.

So long as essential truth is conveyed, there
is almost no limit to the methods which may

be employed.   Single words have more than one meaning, and while the lesser meaning may best teach the child, the larger meaning may best teach the man.   The word " day," in the history of creation in Genesis, does not necessarily mean a day of twenty-four hours, for the prophet Zechariah (14:7) speaks of "days known to the Lord, not day nor night," and the six days of creation may be age-long periods of time.

Christ ordinarily lets men tell their own story.   There was once a cold-blooded murder in Florence.   Differing accounts of it were given by the murderer and by his victim, by the prosecuting counsel and by the pope.   Robert Browning makes all these witnesses describe the matter in " The Ring and the Book."   We are left to make up our own minds about the facts, after the reading of these differing reports; but we do not, on that account, doubt that there occurred a real murder.   Shall we doubt the death of Christ, because the evangelists do not precisely agree as to the superscription on his cross?

King Arthur of the Round Table was a historical character.   But Tennyson, in his Idylls of the King, has made him and his knights the subject of an imaginary story

which will teach great moral truth to the
end of time. Shall we deny the poet's
right to weave round King Arthur a work of
imagination?

Job was also a historical character. Must
we therefore say that the speeches of Job's
friends were also real utterances? Let us
rather regard them as incidents of a poet's
drama.

Shall we refuse to Christ the use of parable
in the case of the prodigal son, or of apologue
in the case of Jonah and of Daniel? These
last are historical characters, mentioned else-
where in Scripture; but it is still possible that
there are legendary incidents in their stories,
and that Jesus himself may have referred to
them as such (Matt. 12:40).

Christ the Sufficient Guarantor of Scripture

Many a modern historian, like H. G. Wells,
quotes varying reports of a battle like Water-
loo, or of an important piece of legislation like
that of Spain in the Netherlands, and we do
not deny him the privilege. If he who ante-
dated Moses gives us varied reports of Moses
and his law, and leaves us to judge between
them, shall we say that there was no Moses
and no law? All these sceptical objections fall

to the ground when we remember that he who permitted these methods of literary composition was himself the Truth, and that he took these humble ways only to impress the truth more readily and more forcibly upon the minds of men.

Remember who Christ was, the manifested God, the one and only medium of God's revelation, and we shall see that the whole Old Testament was composed under his superintendence and so cannot be " broken " up into fragments (John 10: 35). Isaiah " saw his glory, and spoke of him " (John 12: 41); and the same Jesus, who had " many things to say " which his disciples could not bear while he was with them, could " bring to their remembrance all that he had said unto them," and actually did this in John's gospel (16: 12 and 14: 26).

This superintendence of Christ makes the written word, with all its literary and human shortcomings, an expression of the eternal Word, and gives it unity, sufficiency, and authority, as a rule of faith and practice (*Miscellanies,* 1: 251-260).

V

INTERPRETATION OF SCRIPTURE

ONLY the believer's union with Christ gives him possession of Christ's Spirit, and enables him properly to interpret Scripture. This is only to say that he who inspired the Bible can best explain its meaning.

Let us grant at once that there is a wisdom higher than the wisdom of this world, a " wisdom among those who are full-grown," as Paul declares, though it is " God's wisdom in a mystery " (1 Cor. 2: 6, 7).

Our experience of union with Christ enables us to understand Paul's theology, as no merely critical or literary art could do. For Paul takes Christ's own point of view. He is lifted up with Christ into God's eternity. For a time he possesses the normal independence of the human spirit, and its freedom from the limitations of space and time.

Paul can see all human history unrolled before him; can see long processes condensed in their causes; in Adam's one act of sin all humanity is involved; and in Christ's atonement are included all satisfaction to the divine holiness and all provision for the salvation of men. As our Lord could truly say upon the cross: " It is finished " (John 19:30), Paul could also say: " Through one act of righteousness the free gift came unto all men to justification of life " (Rom. 5 : 18).

Christ the Key to the Understanding of the Bible

So I hold that the only key to Paul's meaning, and to the meaning of the entire Scripture, is to be found in Christ, as the preëxistent Word of God, and as God manifested in space and time. As we are creatures of space and time, God in Christ has made himself a creature of space and time, in order that we may know him, love him, and be like him. Whatever Christ is or does, God is and does. In Christ, God himself dies for me, a sinner; for death is only his change from one form of being to another, or from bodily to spiritual manifestation. In Christ's cross, I see myself, as part of the whole redeemed church, to have paid the penalty of sin, and to have emerged from death forever; so that I am now risen with him, and seated with him in " the heavenlies," which are only the antechamber of heaven itself (Eph. 1 : 20; 2 : 7; *Miscellanies,* 1 : 460-471).

The Eternal Word and the Written Word

Let me sum up what I have said by repeating the words with which I began: The written word is the expression of the eternal Word. It is, like the eternal Word, the revelation of God in human forms and methods, but so pervaded by the divine Spirit that, when taken in its entirety and when properly interpreted, it is superior to all merely human teachings.

Scripture teaches, not how the heavens go, but how to go to heaven; it does not teach us physical science, but it "makes us wise unto salvation" (2 Tim. 3:15). With this understanding of its object, if I can only find out what is the testimony of Scripture, I have a divine guide for my earthly way and I can replace my guesses by certainties. But it needs the same Spirit of Christ that inspired it to teach me its true meaning.

The Bible was not given for scholars alone but for common men; and common men as well as scholars have the promise of the Holy Spirit. So the general consent of believers as to the meaning of Scripture is of more account than the surmises of critics, and the creeds and hymnology of the church are a better guide to truth than are all the conclusions of philosophers.

God has "magnified his word above all his name" (Ps. 138:2) by making the Bible, in its unity, a sufficient and authoritative rule of faith and practice. Men may mistake God's meaning; the Bible corrects their errors. Christ is "made unto us wisdom" (1 Cor. 1:30), and his wisdom is better than all the wisdom of this world.

Interpreting the Bible a Solemn Responsibility

What then is the Bible? It is the personal message of the personal God to each one of us as persons, and by our personal treatment of it we are to be judged at the last day.

I cannot shift my personal responsibility upon the critics and hide behind their utterances. When Jenny Geddes, in Old St. Giles of Glasgow, threw her three-legged stool at the minister who was introducing a papal liturgy, she was only asserting her duty to interpret the Bible for herself.

That Bible carries with it its own demonstration of genuineness and authority. In it we see the pictured struggle of the eternal Word to express himself in human methods and forms, beginning with childlike teaching addressed to the infant race, conveying truth by symbol, type, ritual, legislation, as men were able to bear it, stemming the tide of evil by providential interposition and apocalyptic prophecy, furnishing the key to all the past by the incarnation of the Word and his completed atonement, with promise of a completed understanding of that atonement through the teaching of his apostles. What Jesus " began both to do and to teach " (Acts 1 : 1) he finished by the work of Paul and of John, so that we have through them " the faith *once for all* delivered unto the saints; " so that to this completed Bible, in the foresight of Christ, the last of its chapters might close with a warning appropriate to the whole: " If any man shall add unto them, God shall add unto him the plagues which are written in this book " (Rev. 22 : 18, 19).

God's Revelation in the Bible a Final One

As Christ's atonement was finished upon the Cross, so his teaching was finished in the works of Paul and of John, for they were only organs of the posthumous Christ. What Jesus himself taught when here in the flesh was only the introductory lectures of his theological course, to be expounded and explained after his death and resurrection, by his apostles. To them, then, we must go to learn the full meaning of his teaching.

"Is the teaching of Paul or of John as authoritative as that of the incarnate Jesus?" "More so!" we reply, for what Paul and John taught was the posthumous teaching of the Lord himself.

So the earlier utterances of these same apostles are to be interpreted by the later. Paul's "God sent forth his son" (Gal. 4:4), is to be explained by Paul's fuller statement in Ephesians and Colossians, and the fourth gospel is to be regarded as Christ's own rendition of his acts and words when here in the flesh. The Deity and Preëxistence of Christ assure to us the historicity of the gospel according to John (see my "*Books of N. T.*," 117-142), while the human methods of Old Testament teaching find their sufficient explanation in the limitations of him who "emptied himself, taking the form of a servant, being made in the likeness of men" (Phil. 2:7).

Neither Athanasius nor Augustine, Martin Luther or John Calvin, John Bunyan or John Knox, have ever been able to add one jot or tittle to the truth contained in Scripture, but have rather gloried in the fact that they were only media for its circulation.

We may therefore well believe that the superintendence of Christ makes the written

word, with all its literary and human shortcomings, a complete and final expression of the
Eternal Word, and gives it unity, sufficiency
and authority as our rule of faith and practice
(see *Miscellanies,* 1:251-260; 288-303; 478-
493).

Christ the Christian's Authority

In all this chapter on the Interpretation of
Scripture I claim to make Christ himself my
sole authority. If there is philosophy here, it
is a philosophy that antedates any philosophy
of this world, though all that is genuine in
modern philosophy is only a partial rediscovery
of the philosophy which Christ has taught
through Paul and John.

So I hold that in a larger view of Christ, as
he is revealed in Scripture, is the only means
of reconciling our fundamentalists with our
higher critics. I would prefer the word " lit-
eralists " to the word " fundamentalists," for
the trouble with the so-called fundamentalists
is that they are not fundamental enough; they
do not get down to the rock-foundation, the
omnipresent and eternal Christ, who has supervised in past ages the evolution of Scripture,
so that it represents himself in all the forms of
human composition.

The trouble with the " higher critics," so-called, is that they are not high enough to see that same eternal and omnipresent Christ who in Scripture represents himself as the only life and light of men.

They can spell, but they have not yet learned to read. They can, with a telescope, see a fly on a barn-door a half-mile off, but they cannot see the door. They analyze the rind of the orange, but they throw away its contents. They need to look at the Bible *as a whole,* and to see in it the organizing and unifying Spirit of Christ. Personal experience of union with Christ would lift them out of the region of petty criticism into a larger and sounder judgment, and would enable them to see the written word as the final and complete expression of the Eternal Word of God.

Reconciliation between these two sincere but imperfectly informed parties in controversy can come only through a new surrender to Christ. " For he is our Peace, who made both one, and brake down the middle-wall of partition . . . that he might create, *in himself,* of the two, one new man, so making peace " (Eph. 2 : 14, 15).

VI

THE ATONEMENT

WE have reached the point of view from which we must regard the Atonement. Let us strip the doctrine of all materialistic implications, and let us remember that God is essentially *spirit*. Apart from Christ, he has no form or body.

As spirit, independent of space and time, God, with all his attributes of knowledge, love and power, can make himself manifest when and where he will. In Christ, the divine Being is present in every atom of the universe, in every pulsation of my body, in every exercise of my will, and in every movement of human history.

The only qualification we have a right to make is this: the human will has granted to it a delegated power, which can resist the divine will, and can use God's forces and impulses for the production of evil, as the motorman can direct, though he does not furnish, the force that propels his car.

Christ's Natural Oneness with the Sinner

But Christ, as the life of the universe, is the life of humanity; so that the Redeemer is close

64

at hand to redeem, by sharing with the sinner his guilt and misery, and by turning the sinner's enmity into love.

There is a natural union of Christ with all humanity, which precedes and prepares the way for his union with all believers. Whatever is due to the sinner falls upon Christ, to whom he is joined by a tie of life so close as to free it from all charge of book-keeping or external transfer.

When we give ourselves to Christ, and Christ gives himself to us, not only do all our needs become his, but also all his resources become ours. Since Christ is God, the whole Godhead died for me on the cross, as absolutely as if I were the only being to be saved. In receiving Christ, I make the whole Godhead my own, and can say: " Thou are *my* God " (Ps. 31: 14).

With these preliminary remarks, let us see what union with Christ implies in the way of atonement and of salvation. I sum it all up in saying that it implies giving and taking, on the part of God, and also giving and taking on the part of the believer.

What Christ's Oneness with the Believer Implies

When God interpenetrates our life with his

own in Christ, he gives his all to us.   The infinite One so joins us to himself, that all things become ours (1 Cor. 3:22); that is, "all things that pertain unto life and godliness" (2 Pet. 1:3) "shall be added unto us," if we "seek first his kingdom and his righteousness" (Matt. 6:33).

In Christ, God gives himself to us, more fully than any earthly husband gives himself to his wife; endowing us with all his earthly and heavenly goods, and cleaving to us in a union which death cannot part.

But in Christ, God *takes,* as well as gives. Think what is meant by *love,* and you will perceive that God must be an atoning Savior. For love not only gives its all to the object of its affection, but it so identifies itself with that object, as to *share* all its burdens and sorrows and sins. The whole weight of our guilt and penalty falls upon him who is our life, and he bears all for us. "Blessed be the Lord God who daily beareth our burden," says the Psalmist (Ps. 68:19); "In all their affliction he was afflicted," says Isaiah (63:9).

But the New Testament makes this more plain, when it tells us of the Lamb of God, who *takes,* and so "*takes away,* the sins of the world " (John 1:29). Love not only gives, but also takes; gives all its own good, and takes all the other's guilt and pain and need. This is the Christian doctrine of the Atonement. God was in Christ, reconciling himself to the world, and the world to himself. " Him who knew no sin he made to be sin on our behalf, that we might become the righteousness of God in him " (2 Cor. 5:21). If critics had only seen the Atonement as a fact of life, all their objections to its vicarious element, as a matter of book-keeping, would have vanished. If Christ is our life, if all we have and are is derived from him, and if he is God manifest in the flesh, but essentially independent of space and time, then the Atonement is a *biological necessity.*

What the Believer's Oneness with Christ Implies

But I have not yet exhausted the meaning of the Cross. The *salvation of man* as well as the suffering of God was " finished " there. The believer gives and takes, as well as his Savior.

The whole appropriation of salvation by the redeemed was assured and condensed in that one act of God's righteousness. The Father saw our faith as a result of his work on our behalf Predestination and human reception of salvation were joined together in one timeless event, that left no room for contradiction between them.

And the faith that appropriates what Christ is and what Christ has done, is a giving as well as a taking, and a taking as well as a giving. We give all to Christ, in a complete consecration, and we take all from him, by an appropriating faith.

So our salvation is delivered from the charge of an unmoral reliance upon the work of another, by showing itself to be the surrender of our very life to him who is the only source of moral life, to be moulded and fashioned into his likeness.

So our salvation is relieved of the charge that it makes us the slaves of another will, by showing that it is the only way to make us free; since in union with Christ we receive the very fullness of God to energize and gladden us. By union with Christ, the principle of the Atonement, in all its giving and taking, is inwrought into our hearts and lives, so that we, like Paul, " fill up that which is behind of the sufferings of Christ, for his body's sake, which is the church " (Col. 1: 24).

Atonement and Holiness

The necessity of the Atonement, however, cannot be fully appreciated, until we see its relation to the holiness of God. " It must needs be that Christ should suffer," said our Lord (Luke 24:26); and Paul tells us why Christ's suffering was necessary. It was in order " that God *might himself be just*," while at the same time he might be " the justifier of him that hath faith in Jesus " (Rom. 3:26).

Let me repeat in this connection what I have already said. The fundamental attribute of God is holiness, of which justice or righteousness are only forms of manifestation. Holiness is not self-communicating love, but rather, self-affirming righteousness. Holiness limits and conditions love, for love can will happiness, only as happiness results from or consists with righteousness, that is, with conformity to God. All non-conformity to God in moral relations is sin; and sin is hateful in God's sight, for it is the enemy and destroyer of all purity and peace. He therefore attaches suffering to sin, as its proper penalty; though he himself shares in that suffering, because he is the Creator and the life of the sinner.

Christ's suffering, during his earthly life and on the cross, was simply the expression of the age-long suffering of God; indeed, those few hours of agony could not of themselves have redeemed the race, if they had not been the revelation of an eternal fact in the being of God.   Christ accomplishes his atonement through the solidarity of the race, of which he is the life, and so is its representative and surety, justly yet voluntarily bearing its guilt and shame and condemnation as his own (*Systematic Theology,* 2:761).

Christ, therefore, as incarnate, rather *revealed* the Atonement, than made it.   The historical work of atonement was finished upon the cross; but that historical work only revealed to men the Atonement *made both before and after* by the extra-mundane Logos.   The eternal love of God, suffering the necessary reaction of his own holiness against the sin of his creatures and with a view to their salvation,— this is the essence of the Atonement.   God has laid upon Christ the iniquity of us all, and with his stripes we are healed (Is. 53:5, 6); but this is no external transfer of guilt and penalty, but the voluntary suffering of God himself in the person of his Son.

Christ for Us and Christ in Us

Christ must be an *atoning,* in order that he

may be a *cleansing* Savior. Christianity, indeed, is summed up in the two facts: Christ *for* us, and Christ *in* us—Christ *for* us upon the cross, revealing the eternal opposition of holiness to sin, and yet, through God's eternal suffering for sin, making objective atonement for us; and Christ *in* us by his Spirit, renewing in us the lost image of God, and abiding in us as the all-sufficient source of purity and power (*Miscellanies,* 1: 53, 54).

Here we have the two *foci* of the Christian ellipse: given either one, with the smallest fraction of the curve, and you can describe the whole scheme of doctrine.

Let me illustrate these two truths from our American geography. We have two great lakes, Erie and Ontario, and these are connected by the Niagara River, through which Erie pours its waters into Ontario. The whole Christian church throughout the ages has been called the overflow of Jesus Christ, who is infinitely greater than it. Let Lake Erie be the symbol of Christ, the preëxistent Logos, God revealed in the universe. Let Niagara River be to us the picture of this same Christ, now confined to the narrow channel of his manifestation in the flesh, but within those limits showing the same eastward current and downward gravitation which men perceived so imperfectly before. The tremendous cataract, with its waters plunging into the abyss and shaking the very earth, is the suffering and death of the Son of God, which for the first time make palpable to human hearts the forces of righteousness and love operative in the divine nature from the beginning. The law of universal life has been made manifest; now it is seen that justice and judgment are the foundations of God's throne; that God's righteousness everywhere and always makes penalty to follow sin; that the love which creates and upholds sinners must itself be numbered with the transgressors and must bear their iniquities. Niagara has demonstrated the gravitation of Lake Erie. For from Niagara there widens out another peaceful lake. Ontario is the offspring and likeness of Erie. So redeemed humanity is the overflow of Jesus Christ; but only of Jesus Christ after he has passed through the measureless self-abandonment of his earthly life and of his tragic death on Calvary. As the waters of Lake Ontario are ever fed by Niagara, so the church draws its life from the cross. And Christ's purpose is, not that we should repeat Calvary, for that we can never do, but that we should reflect in ourselves that same onward movement and gravitation toward self-sacrifice which he has revealed as characterizing the very life of God.

I have said that there are two *foci* of the Christian ellipse: Christ *for* us, who redeemed us from the curse of the law by being made a curse for us, and Christ *in* us, the hope of glory, whom the apostle calls " the mystery of the gospel " (*Syst. Theol.* 3: 804, 805). The second of these still waits for my illustration.

We need Christ in us, as well as Christ for us. How shall I, how shall society, find purification and healing within? Let me remind you of what they did at Chicago. In all the world there was no river more stagnant and fetid than was Chicago River. Its sluggish stream received the sweepings of the watercraft and the offal of the city, and there was no current to carry the detritus away. There it settled, and bred miasma and fever. At last it was suggested that by cutting through the low ridge between the city and the Desplaines River, the current could be set running in the opposite direction, and drainage could be secured into the Illinois River and the great Mississippi. At a cost of fifteen millions of dollars the cut was made, and now all the water of Lake Michigan can be relied upon to cleanse that turbid stream. What Chicago River could never do for itself, the great lake now does for it.

So no human soul can purge itself of its sin; and what the individual cannot do, humanity at large is powerless to accomplish. Sin has dominion over us, and we are foul to the very depths of our being, until with the help of God we break through the barrier of our self-will, and let the floods of Christ's purifying life flow into us. Then, in an hour, more is done to renew, than all our efforts for years had effected.

Thus humanity is saved, individual by individual, not by philosophy, or philanthropy, or self-development, or self-reformation, but simply by being filled, in Christ, with all the fullness of God (*Syst. Theol.* 3 : 804,805; *Misc.,* 1 : 191-195).

The Appeal of the Cross

In the Cross of Christ, therefore, we see God's whole revelation to men summed up, and thrust upon us for our reception or rejection.

In that Cross are condensed and expressed his character of holiness and of love, his judgment upon sin and his provision for the salvation of the sinner, his suffering in and with his creatures and his sacrificial offering in their behalf.

When God, in the person of his Son, dies of a broken heart for me, a sinner, I feel his appeal to my own heart to be unspeakably affecting. If I resist that appeal, I show myself to be the chief of sinners and to deserve nothing but death. For Christ's Cross reveals not only the greatness of our sin and the greatness of God's love, but it opens to us the whole meaning of human history, the whole secret of the universe, the whole purpose of God when he laid the floor of the firmament with its mosaic of constellations and bade the curtain of night and chaos to rise at the creation (John 3:16; 16:9; Eph. 1:10). Well may the apostle Paul say: " God forbid that I should glory, save in the Cross of our Lord Jesus Christ!" (Gal. 6:14).

VII

UNION WITH CHRIST

T HE degeneration of sin is to be overcome
only by regeneration from above. The
initial work of Christ's Spirit is fortu-
nately instantaneous, though its consequences
are lifelong and unspeakably blessed. We can
turn over a new leaf in a moment; and, whatever may be our past, we can turn to God to-
day, if we will only hear his voice and harden
not our hearts.

Union with Christ by Faith

God regenerates, only by leading us to accept
Christ as our Lord and Savior. Repentance
and faith are the evidences in us that, having
come to him, he has been faithful to his promise, and has not cast us out. Let us make sure
that we know what is meant by faith. It is not
simply an idea of the intellect or a stirring of
the feelings. It is primarily an *act of the will*
(*Syst. Theol.*, 3 : 838, 839).

If I stood upon an islet in the middle of a
rushing river at flood-tide, when there was
danger that a rise in the water might sweep me

away, the sight of a boat near by would be a very pleasant one. But seeing the boat will not save me, nor will my deeply feeling its value as a means of deliverance. Only my getting into the boat will avail when the stream rises to wet my feet.

So faith is not my intellectual belief that there is a Christ, nor any deep stirring of any emotions with regard to him, but only the act of my will in committing myself to him as my Lord and Savior. Obedience and reception, consecration and appropriation, giving and taking, are the essence of faith.

In other words, faith is an act of the will, more than it is an act of intellect or of emotion, and is the means of salvation, not because it is of any value in itself, but only because it joins us to Christ, our manifested God and Redeemer.

Many years ago a man who had lost a beautiful daughter wrote to me of an incident in her early life. The father was building a new house for himself and was inspecting its cellar. As yet there was no stairway, and he was there in the dark. He heard the patter of little feet over his head and he ran to the opening which the stairs were to fill. He heard a little voice ask: " Papa, are you there? " He answered:

"Yes, Mary, I am here. Jump down and I
will catch you." And the little child jumped
down so quickly that if he had not sprung forward to receive her she would have broken her
limbs upon the floor below. It was a leap into
the dark. But she knew her father's voice, and
had faith in his word.

Faith in Christ is, in like manner, a leap in
the dark. But it is the most rational act of
one's life; for it takes for granted that "as a
father pities his children, so the Lord pities
those who fear him" (Ps. 103 : 13), and that,
when we cast ourselves upon Christ for salvation, we shall find "the eternal God to be our
refuge, and underneath us shall be the everlasting arms" (Deut. 33 : 27).

At the first World's Fair ever held in
America, there was exhibited a steam-engine,
all of whose working parts were made of glass.
The steam came from without; but, being hot
enough to move machinery, this steam was
itself invisible, and there was presented the
curious spectacle of an engine, transparent,
moving, and doing important work, while yet
no cause for this activity was perceptible. So
the Christian, the church, humanity, the universe, are in constant and progressive movement; but the Christ, who moves them, and

who furnishes all their power for the good,
though not for the evil, is himself invisible.

The Duty and Depth of this Union

The merging of ourselves in Christ is therefore *the first duty of man.* " This is the work
of God, that ye believe on him whom he hath
sent," says Christ (John 6:29); " for, apart
from me, ye can do nothing" (15:5). But
this merging of ourselves in Christ is not
pantheistic, but rather, the normal assertion of
the human will, and the only way to recover its
freedom. For this reason all those interpreta-
tions of Paul and of John which make our
relation to Christ to be one of mere pupilage
or fellowship fail to get at the secret of the
gospel, which is " Christ *in you,* the hope of
glory " (Col. 1:27).

Union with Christ is *not a union of mere
pupilage or fellowship.* When Paul tells us
that it is no longer he that lives, but that Christ
lives in him (Gal. 2:20), when he speaks of
" Christ who is our life " (Col. 3:4), when he
says, " For me to live is Christ " (Phil. 1:21),
he can only be understood as meaning that the
life of the personal Redeemer subjugates and
penetrates his own. And this is only what we
might expect when we consider that he is al-

ready the natural life of all mankind, the incarnate head of the human race, " the root " as well as " the offspring of David " (Rev. 22 : 16), standing at the door of every human heart, and asking only its assent to enter in and dwell there forever (Rev. 3 : 20).

> " Thou seemest human and divine,
> The highest, holiest manhood, thou;
> Our wills are ours, we know not how;
> Our wills are ours, to make them thine."

The Fruits of this Union

This union with Christ, as a method of salvation, shows its incomparable superiority to all other methods, by giving to the believer *peace, purity and power.* We call the making of peace with God, by the name of Justification. What no pretense of good works could do, the confession of sin and absolute trust in Christ does do, in restoring peace to the conscious sinner. I have One who has paid my debts and answered for me to the offended majesty of God, and since Christ is my very life, his answer is my own.

> " From whence this fear and unbelief?
> Hast thou, O Father, put to grief
> Thy spotless Son for me?
> And will the righteous Judge of men
> Condemn me for that debt of sin
> Which, Lord, was laid on thee?

Turn then, my soul, unto thy rest;
The merits of thy great High Priest
   Speak peace and liberty;
Trust in his efficacious blood
Nor fear thy banishment from God
   Since Jesus died for thee."

" Being justified by faith, we have peace with God, through our Lord Jesus Christ." But, besides Justification, we have Sanctification; by which we mean purification from inward evil, at least in its beginning here, and certainly in its completeness hereafter. Union with Christ secures to the believer the *continuously transforming and assimilating power of Christ's life,*—first, for the soul; secondly, for the body,—consecrating it in the present, and in the future raising it up in the likeness of Christ's glorified body (Phil. 3 : 21).

Here is the real truth of which so-called " Christian Science " has made so perverted a use—the influence of a converted soul on an enervated and sin-stained body.

As Alexander McLaren has said: " If we are *in Christ*, we are like a diver in his crystal bell, and have a solid though invisible wall around us, which keeps all sea-monsters off us, and communicates with the upper air, whence we draw the breath of calm life, and can work in security though in the ocean depths." Many have struggled against sin until they have admitted Christ into their hearts; then they could say: " This is the victory that overcometh the world even our faith " (1 John 5 : 4).

Evolution and Sanctification

Is this doctrine of Union with Christ consistent with any belief in evolution? To this I reply that it is the *only logical conclusion from the theory of theistic evolution.*

If it is consistent with evolution that the physical and natural life of the human race should be derived from a single source, then it is equally consistent with evolution that the moral and spiritual life of the race should be derived from a single source.

Science is now tending toward belief in the origin of humanity in a single pair, and theology is equally drawn to belief in a single transgression as the explanation of man's universal tendencies to evil. Scripture is stating only scientific fact, when it sets the second Adam, the head of redeemed humanity, over against the first Adam, the head of fallen humanity.

We are told that evolution should give us many Christs. We reply that evolution has not given us many Adams. Evolution, as it as-

signs to the natural head of the race a supreme
and unique position, must be consistent with
itself, and must assign a supreme and unique
position to Jesus Christ, the spiritual head of
the race. As there was one Adam from whom
all the natural life of the race was derived, so
there can be but one Christ from whom all the
spiritual life of the race is derived (*Syst.
Theol.,* 3 : 803).

Union with Christ and Mysticism

Our union with Christ is often called a
mystical union. It is indeed inscrutable, since
we cannot fully understand any fact of life.
It is mystical, however, not in the sense of
being unintelligible to the Christian or beyond
the reach of his experience, but only in the
sense of *surpassing in its intimacy and value
any other union of souls that we know*" (Eph.
5 : 32; Col. 1 : 27).

Dr. J. W. Alexander called this doctrine
"the central truth of all theology and of all
religion." The greatest teachers of the church
in modern times, such as Calvin, Bunyan, Edwards, Fuller, have declared it to be their faith.
I may well close my treatment of it with the
rough but thrilling words of Luther: " By faith
thou art so glued to Christ that of thee and him

there becomes as it were one person, so that with confidence thou canst say: ' I am Christ,— that is, Christ's righteousness, victory, *etc.,* are mine;' and Christ in turn can say: ' I am that sinner,—that is, his sins, his death, *etc.,* are mine, because he clings to me and I to him, for we have been joined through faith into one flesh and bone.' " (*Syst. Theol.,* 3 :803, 808).

VIII

THREE IMPUTATIONS

I HAVE reserved until now my treatment of what I regard as the point in theology which most needs explanation, and which I conceive that I have been the first to explain. My explanation is so bound up with my own personal experience, that I could not easily give it without mention of the steps by which I reached it. I have hope that, as I tell of my own way of coming to the knowledge of the truth, others may be led to follow me.

Three imputations are declared in Scripture as essential to evangelical doctrine. They are, first, the imputation of Adam's sin to the whole human race; secondly, the imputation of all human sin to Christ; and, thirdly, the imputation of Christ's merits and righteousness to the believer.

Each one of these imputations seems at first sight to involve a sort of legal fiction,—the crediting to one party of what belongs exclusively to another; an arbitrary treatment of wholly moral issues; an external transfer, either of guilt or of righteousness. When the federal theology explained all this upon the ground of God's covenant with Adam and with Christ, it seemed to involve God in a merely forensic process, to make him a God of expedients, to reduce divine justice to bookkeeping, to ignore all truth and reality in God.

I was brought up in that system of thought. The preaching to which I listened when a child, and the instruction of the theological seminary which I afterward received, emphasized the doctrine of the Covenants, and answered objections by referring the objector to the unsearchable wisdom or sovereignty of God.

First Phase of Experience

My conversion did not awaken doubts since it ignored all doctrine, except the doctrines of sin and salvation. If ever there was a purely Arminian or Pelagian conversion, mine was such an one.

I was one of a rather brilliant and hilarious set of students at Yale. We were not openly vicious, but we were selfishly ambitious, and on the verge of a moral precipice. The timely word of a classmate set me thinking. I saw that I must change, or die.

During a college vacation, at my own home, I found myself at a revival meeting, under the eagle eye of Charles G. Finney, the evangelist. He seemed to speak directly to me, when he said: " If there is any one here who sees that he ought to forsake his sins and to serve God, let him rise and go into the inquiry room, and some one will tell him what to do." So I arose and went out. A minister of the Gospel met me, and asked me if I would begin from that hour to serve God, looking to him to show me the way. After much hesitation, I told him that I would, and I went home in the dark, thinking all the way that I was very foolish, yet determined to begin a new life from that day.

I began to read my Bible. I began to pray. But though I sought God, I did not find him until, some weeks after returning to college, bowed down with a new sense of sin and need, I read the verse in 2 Cor. 6: 17, 18, " Wherefore come ye out from among them and be ye separate, saith the Lord, and touch not the unclean thing, and I will receive you, and will be a Father to you, and ye shall be my sons and daughters, saith the Lord Almighty." Then I said to myself: " That is *I;* God is my Father and friend!" And for the first time in my life I felt that there was a tie that bound me to God. I looked out through the elms to the stars that shone that evening, and I knew that when those stars should grow pale and die, the eternal God would be my refuge, and underneath me would be the everlasting arms.

I have narrated this experience not as cause of self-gratulation, but to show how meagre an apprehension of truth may consist with a real turning to God. For if ever I was converted, that decision marked my conversion. The peculiarity of it was, that in it I had absolutely no sense that the change in me was in any way due to the influence of the Holy Spirit, or had been made possible by the work of Christ.

Except for the fact that I had a sort of traditional and theoretical belief in these things, in the background of my consciousness, my conversion might have been a purely Unitarian or agnostic reliance upon the love and truth of God. This fact makes me tolerant of Unitarian Christianity, though I now recognize it as an infantile faith, like that of Peter, James and John on the banks of the Jordan, when they followed Jesus without knowing anything about his deity or his atonement.

Second Phase of Experience

But the faith of my conversion did not suffice for my subsequent life and ministry, and I must tell of a second stage in my experience. I entered the theological seminary, and there encountered the full strain upon my faith of the federal thology. I was docile and determined to believe, but I suspended judgment, and waited for further light. I was accepted by an ordaining council and admitted to the ministry.

I could preach about sin, and I could say that God would forgive the penitent, but the way of salvation I knew little of. I found Jordan a hard road to travel. I was conscientious, and I worked myself almost to death. But the more I worked, the weaker and more helpless I seemed. A universe of evil influences seemed to be fighting against me. People were converted, but I was constantly losing strength and heart. I began to think myself past feeling, and that God had taken his Holy Spirit from me.

Was I indeed a Christian at all? And had I not been deceived in thinking I had ever turned to God? In utter despair of myself, I determined to devote my whole summer vacation to learning where I stood before God, to read nothing but the Bible, and to give up the ministry if I did not find peace.

Then God *revealed his Son in* me, as he did

in the apostle Paul (Gal. 1:16). I read in the
Acts that the early Christians were filled with
joy and with the Holy Spirit. I read the closing chapters of John's gospel, and I learned the
secret of their strength and gladness, even the
mystery of the gospel, " which is *Christ in you,
the hope of glory*" (Col. 1:27).

My conversion had been, all unconsciously to
myself, the entrance of Christ into my soul;
but only now did I learn that he had joined
himself to me in a union which death could not
part, and had taken me to be his partner in his
work of men's salvation. I had only to abide
in him, and have him abiding in me, and I
should be able to do great things in his name
(John 15:4). The God to whom I had sur-
rendered at my conversion proved to be Christ
my Savior; and since in him was all the fulness
of the Godhead, all things were practically
mine (Col. 2:9; 1 Cor. 3:22).

Instead of facing a universe of evil influences, I had all the powers of heaven and
earth to back me up, and to make me " mighty
through God" to bring to naught fortresses
of evil. No least effort of mine should be in
vain (1 Cor. 15:58).

I went back to my church as a conqueror. I
preached on Union with Christ as the central

thought of all theology and of all religion. Christians came to me saying with tears: " We never heard this before." There followed in that congregation many conversions almost as wonderful as that of Saul on the way to Damascus. And I learned my first lesson in the matter of imputations. My federalism was succeeded by a *realistic theology.*

Imputation is grounded in union, not union in imputation. Because I am one with Christ, and Christ's life has become my life, God can attribute to me whatever Christ is, and whatever Christ has done.

The relation is *biological,* rather than forensic. I can, on my part, share in all Christ's suffering, and in all Christ's victory. I am lifted up into his eternity, and can take advantage of his acts as fully as if they were my own. So that old tract, " The Seven Togethers," can be justified, as a simple repetition of the teaching of the apostle Paul: I am—

1. Crucified together with Christ (Gal. 2:20);
2. Dead together with Christ (Col. 2:29);
3. Buried together with Christ (Rom. 6:4);
4. Quickened together with Christ (Eph. 2:5);
5. Raised together with Christ (Col. 3:1);
6. Sufferer together with Christ (Rom. 8:17);
7. Glorified together with Christ (Rom. 8:17).

Since Christ is my very life (Col. 3:4), all charge of legal fiction on the part of God disappears; and all charge of immoral appropriation on my own part disappears also, since union with Christ gives me not only his moral status, but also his moral power.

Third Phase of Experience

I make no claim to originality in this discovery, for many so called " mystics " have made it before me. But it transformed my theology none the less, by turning it from a theology of technicalities into a theology of life. It was not long before I saw my way to apply the same general principle to the interpretation of the *relation of the race to its first father*.

In this matter I was helped by the reading of an old book by Baird, entitled " The Elohim Revealed," in which God's imputation of Adam's sin to all his descendants was explained as a simple recognition of their natural inheritance from him of an enfeebled and perverse will. Here I have only added the idea of subliminal tendencies constantly working against the good, tendencies which can be overcome only by God's regenerating Spirit, and have also added the conception of an act in

God's eternity which summed up and judged the whole race of man as one. These two imputations,—that of Christ's righteousness to the believer and that of Adam's sin to the race, —I thought I had solved many years ago. There remained a third instance of imputation which only in late years I have been able to explain. It is the most difficult of all.

To me it has been the greatest problem of theology, how to explain *God's imputation to Christ of the sins of the whole race.* Here I could find no light in any past work of theology. When I privately consulted Dr. Shedd, he could only call it a mystery of God.

I was not satisfied. I wanted to find some union of Christ with humanity which would make this imputation also realistic and biological. I have found it, and have expounded it, in my book entitled, *" Christ in Creation."* It is my chief contribution to scientific theology; and though I claim to have thrown new light on the doctrine of God's law, and of union with Christ, it is by my explanation of God's imputation of all human sin to Christ that my theology must stand or fall.

In the earlier chapters of this *Primer* I have shown that God is expressed and known only in Christ; that Christ is the life of humanity as

well as the life of nature; that the solidarity of
the race, no less than the harmony of the universe, is due to his constant volition; that he
is the source of all good, while our wills are the
source of all evil; that he has taken upon himself the burden of our sins by suffering in us
all our guilt and misery; that in him God has
condemned sin by bearing in himself its consequences; that union with the human race in
Christ has made God the greatest sufferer in
the universe; that this vindication of justice
was due to his moral character of holiness,
and indispensable to human salvation; that
love has paid the penalty of sin by himself
enduring that penalty; that all this was done
in that one " act of righteousness " when the
heart of God was broken on the cross for our
salvation.

Dr. Forsyth uttered a great truth, when he
said that " God laid a *world-sin* upon a *world-
soul.*" But I have gone more nearly to the
heart of the truth, in showing how Christ
becomes the world-soul by being the one and
only manifestation of God in nature and in
humanity.

Here are the reason and the necessity of the
Atonement. He who gives himself to a sinful
humanity, if he be holy, must suffer; and the

suffering of the holy God on account of sin is the essence of the Atonement.

Bronson Alcott, the school-teacher, held out his own hand to be feruled by the boy who had broken the rules of the school. So the cross of Christ is a symbolic declaration that without suffering there could be no remission, but that it was also possible that the blood of the Son of God could atone for the sins of the world.

Alcott's illustration, however, lacks the element of *universality* that belongs to the imputation of our sins to Christ, for it is God's own blood that was shed upon the Cross,

> "When Christ, the mighty Maker, died
> For man, the creature's, sin."

Those who dislike the term "blood-atonement," need to remember that a lower thing is often the preparation and symbol of a higher. We do not think it degrading to eat our lamb-chop of a morning, because it comes from the shambles. When we hear Christ saying: "This cup is the new covenant in my blood" (1 Cor. 11:25), we look forward to the glory that is to be revealed, forgetting the shame by which it was purchased.

That blood was the symbol of Christ's *life*— the life with which he had endowed us at our creation—but which by regeneration and sanctification he has changed into moral life and power.

Shall we not praise him who so shared his life with us as to begin, a microscopic point in the womb of the Virgin, and from that low beginning grew till he " fills all in all " (Eph. 1: 22)?

Shall we not make his shed blood the theme of our earthly song, as they do who surround " the throne of God and of the Lamb that hath been slain " (Rev. 5: 12)?

We read of " the church of God which he purchased with his own blood " (Acts 20: 28); and when we speak of " blood-atonement " we are only declaring the merits of him " who is over all, God blessed forever " (Rom. 9: 5), but who, " for the joy that was set before him, endured the cross, despising the shame " (Heb. 12:2), in order that he " might bring many sons into glory " (Heb. 2: 10). May we, in virtue of God's *third instance of imputation,* " overcome through the blood of the Lamb " (Rev. 12: 11)!

IX

ULTIMATE FATES

THE decision of the will for or against Christ necessarily determines whether the subsequent evolution of the individual shall be an upward or a downward evolution.

If that decision be *for* Christ, there will result an ever increasing measure of knowledge, love, and spiritual power. " If any man willeth to do his will," says our Lord, " he shall know of the teaching " (John 7:17); the love of Christ for him will kindle new love in his heart (2 Cor. 5:14); and the reception of strength from his Master will enable him to do greater things in his service (John 14:12).

On the other hand, *rejection* of Christ will result in progressive deterioration, the blinding of intellect, the deadening of affection, and the weakening of will. The Christless man becomes " vain in his reasonings and his senseless heart is darkened " (Rom. 1: 21). He comes to be " past feeling," either of his own depravity or of the love of God (Eph. 4: 19). His dislike for holy things becomes an open " en-

mity to God " (Rom. 8:7). Refusing regeneration, he becomes a prey to degeneration.

The Evolution of Sin and Death

And so the ultimate fate of the wicked is
suggested by our application to it of the
principle of evolution. I have shown in my
Miscellanies (2: 110-128) that neither annihilation, nor external and positive inflictions, are
warranted by Scripture; while yet we read of
an " eternal sin," and of a punishment worse
than " fire and brimstone " (Mark 3:29; Ps.
11:6; 32:3, 4). As in joining himself to the
will of Christ man receives divine life, joy,
strength—the motor-elements of upward progress—so, in rejecting Christ's will, he loses
even the natural strength with which Christ
had endowed him. An evil and selfish will
becomes more and more hostile to God and
man; loses insight, fellowship, power; ex-
changes free-will for automatic subservience to
impulses from without; in short, reverts to the
animal type from which humanity has been by
Christ's power evolved.

" Man that is in honor, and understandeth
not, is like the beasts that perish " (Ps. 49:20).
God does not punish him, so much as he punishes himself. He does not cease to be; but he

lives, stricken and blasted by his own per-
versity. God " requireth that which is past "
(Eccl. 3 : 15), not by stripes or thunderbolts,
not necessarily by any positive inflictions, but
by the sinner's own memory, conscience, and
character; and these are the essence of hell.

As man came up from the brute, so he can
return to the brute; but " *without* are the
dogs " (Rom. 22 : 15), forever excluded from
God and from the society of the holy. Indeed,
as even the animal creation arose from that
which was inert matter, the spirit that will not
drink of the fountain of life may become at
last little more than mere matter, only active
by pressure from without. He who is too
proud to join himself to Christ and become
lord of all, may end by losing all that makes
his honor and dignity in the universe, and may
only serve to all worlds and ages as a warning
against sin. So God's love may utilize opposition to his holiness, and may make even the
wicked to serve him. Refusing Christ, the
sinner may himself become the refuse of the
universe, scrapped and cast off forever (*Systematic Theology,* 3 : 1035-1056).

The Evolution of Salvation

What *heaven* is really to be, may also appear

from a consideration of this principle of progress. Joining ourselves to Christ, we determine an upward evolution, and participate in God's knowledge, love and dominion.

"In thy light shall we see light" (Ps. 36:9). "He that loveth me shall be loved of my Father" (John 14:21). "We have waited for him, and he will save us" (Is. 25:9; 63:1). "Ye also shall sit upon twelve thrones, judging the twelve tribes of Israel" (Matt. 19:28). "Know ye not that we shall judge angels?" (1 Cor. 6:3). "Things which eye saw not, and ear heard not, and which entered not into the heart of man, whatsoever things God prepared for them that love him" (1 Cor. 2:9). "For all things are yours" (1 Cor. 3:21). "Filled unto all the fullness of God" (Eph. 3:19).

Thus is held out to us the prospect of an eternal growth in the wisdom, favor, and lordship of the infinite God. And this infinite God is none other than the crucified but now risen Savior, who begs us to admit him to our hearts (Rev. 3:20).

The Crowning of the Redeemer

As all things have been created by the power and for the honor of our great Redeemer (Col. 1 : 16), it is no narrow service to which we give ourselves when we surrender ourselves to Christ. " On his head are many crowns " (Rev. 19 : 12) ; the crown of literature and the crown of art, the crown of science and the crown of philosophy, the crown of unfettered industry and the crown of democratic government (*Miscellanies,* 1 : 210-219).

At the feet of him who was crowned with thorns shall be cast the crowns of all the saved, from all the continents and from all the islands of the sea. Mongolia and Polynesia and Patagonia shall join in stretching forth their hands with offerings to Christ. A multitude that no man can number shall praise him of those who have been redeemed from the earth.

But why should we limit the praise to the inhabitants of this little sphere? Is it not written that God will " sum up all things in Christ, the things in the heavens " as well as " the things upon the earth " (Eph. 1 : 10) ; that " to principalities and powers in heavenly places shall be made known his manifold wisdom " (Eph. 3 : 10) ; that " in the name of Jesus every knee shall bow, of things in heaven " as well as on earth and under the earth (Phil. 2 : 10) ? May we not believe, with Mark Hopkins, that, in the great day of resti-

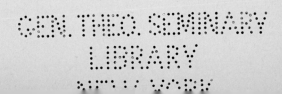

tution, other intelligences will come in long procession from other departments of the universe, "great white legions from Sirius and Arcturus and the chambers of the South," to bow the knee and to confess that Jesus Christ is Lord?

"When Shall These Things Be?"

Is that day near, or is it far away? We are reminded of the controversy between the pre-millennialists and the post-millennialists. I am persuaded that a careful study of Scripture will show that each of these views has its element of truth, and that with some qualifications we may admit both into our scheme of doctrine.

For a complete statement of my faith in this important matter I must refer to my *Systematic Theology* (3:1013-1014). But I venture to summarize what I there teach, and to preface that summary with three general remarks: first, that Christ's manifestations are primarily spiritual and invisible, and only afterwards are visible and physical; secondly, that Scripture and the history of the church show that this priority of the spiritual in Christ's manifestations was the faith of the early apostles and their disciples; and thirdly, that we may

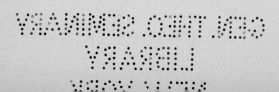

reasonably expect that Christ's final manifestation of himself will follow the same rule of spirituality first, and physical impressiveness afterwards.

Inward Realizations and Outward Manifestations

In my book entitled "*A Tour of the Missions*," 2nd ed., 276-289, I have called attention to the oneness of human nature. Man is both soul and body, spiritual and physical. The redemption of one part of him is the guaranty of the redemption of the other. The prophet is lifted up to see in germinal spiritual life the certainty also of final spiritual perfection, in resurrection of the soul the resurrection of the body.

There are four separate instances in which this priority of the spiritual appears. There is, first, a *spiritual death* ("dead through your trespasses and sins" Eph. 2:1); but secondly a *physical and literal death* ("This is the second death, even the lake of fire," Rev. 20:14). First, again, there is a *spiritual judgment* (Is. 26:9; John 3:13; 12:31); but secondly, an *outward and literal judgment* (Acts 17:31). First, there is an *invisible and spiritual coming of Christ* (Matt. 16:28; John

14: 16, 18 and John 14: 3) ; but afterwards, a
final, visible, and literal coming (Matt.
25: 31). So also, first, a *spiritual resurrection,*
already in some cases accomplished (John
5: 25,—" the hour cometh, and *now is* ") ; but
also a *physical and literal resurrection* (John
5: 28, 29,—" The hour cometh, in which all
that are in the tombs shall hear his voice ").
So we may regard " the first resurrection " in
Rev. 20: 8 as spiritual and invisible, while the
second resurrection, mentioned in verse 13
which follows, is clearly visible.

In other words, Christ's second coming is
both of these: it is *pre-millennial spiritually,*
but *post-millennial physically and visibly.* At
the beginning of the thousand years of conquest
and success, Christ comes to his church in
mighty reinforcement of its spiritual energies.
At the end of a thousand years of peace and
progress, Christ comes to his church visibly
and literally, in the clouds of heaven, with
power and great glory, to reward his faithful
followers and to put an end to the opposition
of his foes.

The Priority of the Spiritual

This first pre-millennial coming by his Spirit
seems needed, to make the second coming in-

telligible or possible. When the fullness of time had come, God sent forth his Son; for without spiritual preparation of the world in the knowledge of its sin, the first coming of Christ in the flesh would not have manifested God. So the fullness of time must come, before Christ can manifest himself literally and visibly in his second coming; for without spiritual preparation the church will not be able to understand his manifestation.

What would be the use of Christ's visible advent to a dead church? Unbelievers cannot understand a spiritual kingdom. When Saul was smitten to the earth on his way to Damascus, that light of Christ's manifestation, brighter than the sun, came to a man already under the influence of the convicting Spirit and kicking against the pricks of conscience (Acts 26: 14). So he could understand Christ's manifestation. But those who were with him were perfectly blind to its meaning: "they heard the voice, but they beheld no man" (Acts 22: 9). There must first be a believing church, or Christ's visible coming will be in vain.

So the visible coming is preceded by an invisible coming, and this is pre-millennial. When the church arises and shines because her Light is come invisibly, then he who is the

Light personified will come in power and glory, and that coming will be post-millennial. Our duty, then, is not to expect a speedy second advent in the clouds of heaven, but to pray for a mighty coming of Christ in the hearts of his apathetic and slumbering people, rousing them to trust his promise and to conquer the world.

But the internal is not all. Body and soul go together. Christ is the Savior of the body also, and when he is manifested, then we shall be manifested with him in glory (Col. 3:4). But that shall be after, and not before, the spiritual victory has been won.

Pre-millennialism, when it means the immediate end of the present dispensation and the sudden dawn of the day of judgment, is often the cause of half-heartedness in Christian enterprise. Why work in the vineyard, when the Master may come before the harvest? But Pre-millennialism, when it means the spiritual coming of Christ, to refresh and strengthen his army for conflict and victory, is an incentive to the most vigorous and enthusiastic effort. Let us be pre-millennialists of the latter sort.

The Glorious Completion of Salvation

Let us be post-millennialists also: I fear that

many who object to Pre-millennialism have really *lost faith in any literal and visible coming of Christ*. The gradual spread of Christian truth is enough for them, and they give a purely spiritual interpretation to all promises of Christ's manifestation. I will not say that these brethren have given up all faith in the inspiration of the Scriptures, but their conception of inspiration is a very different one from mine. And when Scripture teaches of a coming of Christ in the clouds of heaven, of the changing of the body of our humiliation into the likeness of his glorified body, and of a new city of God in which dwells righteousness, I cannot think that it is to be interpreted figuratively.

Paul has no manner of doubt about the matter, for he says: "We know that if the earthly house of this tabernacle be dissolved, we have a building from God, a house not made with hands, eternal in the heavens." "For our citizenship is in heaven whence also we wait for a Savior, the Lord Jesus Christ, who shall fashion anew the body of our humiliation, that it may be conformed to the body of his glory, according to the working whereby he is able even to subject all things unto himself" (2 Cor. 5 :1; Phil. 3 :20-21).

So I think that, with Paul, we may be post-millennialists also, expecting that, at Christ's final manifestation of himself at the end of the millennium, " we shall be like him, because we shall see him as he is " (1 John 3:2). Let us pray then for his coming and manifestation in our hearts, that we may be prepared for his coming and manifestation in the world.

X

ETHICAL IMPLICATIONS

IN closing this brief synopsis of doctrine, I cannot omit all allusion to *things that should follow*. The apostle Paul was never content to leave his theology by itself, as if it were a mere play of rhetoric, or an exercise of philosophical speculation. The one word " Therefore," in Rom. 12: 1, shows that, to him, doctrine had more serious consequences. It was the *source of ethics;* and, if it did not lead to ethics, it had no validity or right to be. " The proof of the pudding is in the eating," says an old proverb, and that is true most of all in theology.

I deeply feel the necessity of vindicating my own work by this principle. But here also I feel that my teaching must be more than ever dogmatic and autobiographical. After what I have already taught, I trust the reader will bear with me if I strain his attention and his faith to the utmost limit; for this is no child's play, but a statement of personal relations between the personal God and each individual person whom he has made. As the whole of

God is in every place, this bit of ethics has to
do with your soul, as much as if you and God
were the only persons in the universe. I put
my thought into four great statements:

1. *Here is Something to Believe*

In writing this *Primer* I have had a new
experience. It began with a dream. I seemed
to be in great darkness, and that darkness
seemed to be God's coming down to judgment. His universe seemed to be full of evil;
and he had come to put that evil away, not
by wrath and justice, but by taking it to himself, and bearing all its sin and misery in his
own great heart.

Out of the darkness I heard a mighty word,
and the word was " NOW." I saw a garden,
and a trembling human form. It was God
himself, narrowed down into the person of his
Son. And that frail mortal was drinking the
cup of sorrow and shame, till his sweat and
blood fell in drops to the ground.

Never before had I realized what it was for
the Man of Sorrows to *take upon himself the
sins of the world*. As his heart broke for sorrow, so my heart broke for sympathy, till I
heard the word: "It is finished" (John
19:20). Then came a sudden change, and all

was light. Since Christ had "trodden the winepress alone" (Is. 63:3), the ransom had been paid, the atonement had been made, and the universe was free. It seemed to me as if all the sons of God were shouting for joy. The sound of celestial music met my ears and I awoke.

I am not much of a believer in dreams, though they suggest and revive many good suggestions of the day. But this dream led me to reflection. What was the meaning of that word " NOW " ?

In the dream, I seemed imprisoned in the bonds of space and time. In my sounder sense, I remembered that God is not so imprisoned. I had heard what may really be the language of eternity.

That scene of appropriated suffering was not matter of an hour, a day, or even of a lifetime, but was God's eternal vindication of himself in his treatment of sin.

I saw more clearly than ever that this is God's way of atonement,—not laying the burden and responsibility of it upon man, but providing himself the sacrifice, as he did of old to Abraham (Gen. 22:8-14). " The Lord will provide,"—not merely earthly good, but all good, for the body and for the soul, for time and for eternity. Believe this, and you have solved the problem of the universe, and have learned that God had a right to make you, because he could redeem you.

2. *Here is Something to Confess*

I think no one can really believe what I have written thus far without being moved to confession, both of his own sin, and of God's mercy in his salvation. All idea of comparing his own proud and self-moved righteousness with the holiness of God, is like thrusting an electric lamp against the sun; the astronomer with his smoked glass sees it as a black spot upon that blazing disk. Infinite generosity calls for generous response. Not to feel that one is a sinner, in the presence of such love, is to declare that one is "past feeling" and is doomed to death.

The redeemed soul hungers and thirsts to make his redemption known (Acts 4:20); he cannot stay; he must speak forth the things which he has seen and heard. Non-confession proves lack of belief.

And here is the error of our churches. We seek effects, without thinking of causes. When the seven churches of Asia ceased to be evangelical, they ceased also to be evangelistic; and when they lost their message, they lost also their existence.

We are running the same course of futility: much hole-drilling, but no dynamite; many missionaries, but no Gospel. What we need is to see the Cross anew, as Luther did; to cry: " *Für mich?* " " For me? " as Luther did. Then we, too, could face the Diet of Worms, and brave its terrors, and our work like his would abide.

So I plead for spiritual revival, instead of six-penny socialism, as the only means of present salvation; for internal union with Christ, instead of theatrical effort to bring about an external union with other bodies of Christians.

Come quickly, Lord Jesus! Give us the spirit of confession! Let us pledge ourselves and our institutions, to make evangelical confession not simply possible, as the basis of gifts, but also prerequisite to all our reception and disbursement of funds. So shall we be ourselves confessed, when we meet our Lord in his judgment.

3. *Here is Something to Preach*

Can we doubt that this is the truth that will capture the world? Christ himself did not doubt it. " And I, if I be lifted up, will draw all men unto me," were his own words (John 12:32).

What are we to think of the recent sneers at evangelization, as compared with effort to preach the Gospel? Does it not show that Christian men have lost their faith in that Gospel, and that they are trusting to their own works, instead of trusting to God's appointed method of salvation?

Has not every great missionary conquest begun with the touching of heathen hearts by the story of the Cross? From Greenland to Cape Town, and from China to Peru, that story has done more than any economic benefits to civilize and to reform.

Thank God for hospitals and for schools! But remember that these are *secondary and not primary means of blessing,* and that they may become instruments of evil, unless purified and accompanied by the preaching of the Cross.

I even go so far as to say that, without an experience of the truth of union with Christ, no young man has a right to enter the Christian ministry. It is certain that without such experience he will be as feeble and abashed as I myself was at the beginning of my work. I long to see the day when ordaining councils and presbyteries will refuse to lay hands on students who have no settled faith, and will tell them to go back to Jericho till their beards are grown.

One man with settled faith is worth a hundred who know not where they stand in theology. Red-hot zeal, even with many defects of training, wins more souls to Christ, than do all the modern philanthropies; for it is the Gospel, and not merely its applications, which is " the power of God unto salvation " (Rom. 1 : 16).

4. *Here is Something to Live By, and to Die By*

Was there ever such intensity of effort as that of the Apostle Paul? Read 2 Cor. 11 : 23-28, and remember his shipwrecks and scourgings!

Compare with these the half-heartedness and dilly-dallying of our Christian service,—our men so plainly given to money-making, our women so plainly given to social ambitions outside the church, and only a few laying all their gifts and influence at the feet of Christ, their Lord!

I do not excuse myself, but rather mourn that I have come so far short of the intensity of zeal which ought to characterize every true believer.

> " Lord, it is my chief complaint
>   That my love is weak and faint;
>   Yet I love thee, and adore!
> Oh for grace to love thee more! "

And I close this *Primer* by saying that I would wish to have only two inscriptions on the tablet that preserves my memory. The first is: " For me to live is Christ." And the second is: " I have kept the faith."

Dear Reader, you and I must soon stand at the judgment-seat of Christ. It will be then as if he and you were the only persons in the universe—all his sacrifice endured for you alone—all his revelation in nature and in Scripture made to show you the way of life.

Will you say that you have never seen God? The answer will be that you have never seen anything else, for every atom in the universe has been a manifestation of him.

Will you say that he has never spoken to you? The answer will be that every word of Scripture was his voice to your soul.

The only question then will be that question of the ages: " What think ye of the Christ? Whose son is he? " (Matt. 22:42).

How have you used the talent with which he endowed you? What has been your attitude toward that great movement of the world to God? Have you fallen in with it and promoted it, or have you turned aside, to make your selfish interest supreme?

Will you *now* join yourself to Christ, and so launch your barque on the vast tide that is everywhere flowing toward God, or will you be left high and dry on the shores of time, as the merest refuse of the universe?

In short will you chose to worship Christ, or the works of his hands?

Your answer will determine your real character, and decide your eternal destiny. Christ, or the Universe? Choose you this day whom you will serve!

May your answer be the words of the poet:

"The holy, meek, unspotted Lamb,
   Who from the Father's bosom came
For me and for my sins to atone,
   Him for my Lord and God I own."

May this answer be the result of reading this *Primer of Theology,* in the case of some one who has been led by it to see his own sin and his need of Christ as a Savior! For Christ is near to save, and his words are: " Him that

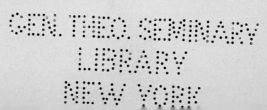

cometh to me, I will in no wise cast out"
(John 6:37).

In the *Pilgrim's Progress,* John Bunyan sees
a man with a muck-rake, who is gathering a
few straws, while a glittering crown hangs, all
unnoticed, over his head. Let us leave the
straws, and take the crown; for "now is the
accepted time; now is the day of salvation"
(2 Cor. 6:2)!